Excerpts from Reviews

"The book, *'Succeeding in Interviews'*, has been written in a very simple and readable manner and will definitely succeed in providing useful tips for Winning Interviews".

Rajan Dutta, Chief of HR & TQM, Escotel Mobile Communications

"I found the book to be very informative and easy to read. It is a *'Bible'* for those who want to excel in interviews".

G P Rao, VP- HR, Birla VXL Ltd.

"There are so many great tips in this book that you can really use for making your career path".

P N Shukla, Group Head – HRD, Escorts Ltd.

"The book, *'Succeeding in Interviews'*, is the result of Mr Subhash Jagota's years of experience which he has shared in the book by giving useful practical guidelines for succeeding in interviews".

Dwarka Nath, President DMA & Director HR, Glaxo Smithkline Beecham

"I would like to congratulate Mr Subhash Jagota for coming up with a winning book once again".

Atul Chauhan, Director, AKC Group of Companies

"It is an interesting book, worth reading.....the author has done an excellent work in drawing out the various aspects of interviews".

S Y Siddqui, Chief HR, New Holland Director

Succeeding in Interviews

SUBHASH JAGOTA

EXCEL BOOKS

Copy Editor
Smita Kulshreshtha

Art Editor
Abha Bhatia

Designer
Shiv Mehta

Publisher
Anurag Jain

ISBN: 81-7446-254-6

First Edition: New Delhi, 2001

EXCEL BOOKS
A-45, Naraina, Phase-I
New Delhi-110028

Published by Anurag Jain for
Excel Books, A-45, Naraina,
Phase-I, New Delhi-110 028 and
Printed at Kumar Offset Printers, Delhi-31

CONTENTS

FOREWORD

'Succeeding in Interviews', is yet another brilliant exposition by Mr Subhash Jagota who is very a well-known corporate figure. In this book, he has conveyed his message of succeeding in interviews in a very simple and practical language. The book has been written in an interesting manner and includes all the aspects that should be taken into account during the interview process.

This book will be very helpful to the readers particularly to the students taking the professional interviews in helping them find the right jobs.

K K AHUJA
Executive Director – HR
Gujarat Heavy Ind Ltd.

ACKNOWLEDGEMENTS

I acknowledge contributions of the following in bringing out this book:

- Organisations where I have worked & gained knowledge like Birla Group, Ballarpur Industries, Escorts, Dabur and Punj Lloyd.
- Wife Veena and my son Kapil for their support and patience and also for giving good ideas.
- I also appreciate contributions of Mohit, Rachna, Puneet, Nidhi, Rohit, Sakul, Sidhant and Shilpa.
- My friends K K Ahuja, D K Bakshi, Rajan Dutta, R K Kapila, K K Ahuja, G P S Chandel and K K Singh for giving me some valuable inputs for the book.

The Publisher Excel Books, especially Anurag Jain for his support and belief.

SUBHASH JAGOTA

Introduction

Organisations are looking for candidates who have positive attitude, fire of enthusiasm, ability and keenness to learn, good team skills, ability to think BIG and grow in the organisation

Introduction

We have ushered into an era where the world is gradually being transformed into a global village. Selecting the right people at the reasonable cost is the key to success. *Today organisations are looking for candidates who have positive attitude, fire of enthusiasm, ability and keenness to learn, good team skills, ability to think BIG and grow in the organisation.* The goal of every interview is to uncover a clear picture of a candidate's past accomplishments and his future potential. The interviewers, with the help of various questions, try to accurately measure past performance and predict the future performance of the candidate. The interviewees, on the other hand, convince the potential recruiter that they are well equipped by virtue of their qualifications, experience, potential, motivation and personality to do the job that they are offered.

There is no magic formula, which will always ensure a successful outcome of an interview, but it is possible to take steps to ensure that you are the one who has the maximum chance of succeeding. Developing adequate skills for appearing in an interview will definitely help you to know what is really required, and how to present yourself to the best possible advantage.

This book will help all job seekers, including students, and those who want to change their jobs or careers, to enhance their interviewing skills and improve their opportunities for employment. The simple guidelines in this book will enable you to quickly differentiate between a haphazard interview, where the candidate does not know what is the difference between success and failure, and a successful interview where the candidate knows exactly what he wants to achieve from the interview and how should he go about it. The book guides you on how to prepare, what sort of information should be collected, and gives many basic pointers on conduct during the interview.

A. *"Before the Interview"*, This chapter focuses on preparation before the interview. Expressing yourself clearly and concisely is a key element of effective interviewing. Self-assessment of your skills, interests will help you to project a positive impression.

B. *"Going for the Interview"*, emphasises the importance of certain aspects such as, punctuality, being polite to everyone you meet.

C. *"Dress for Success"*, gives insights into the importance of dressing up smartly and appropriately for the interview.

D. The subject of *"What to Say, What Not to Say"* reflects the significance of preparing yourself for the questions that may be asked so that you organise your thoughts in order to project a positive impression.

Nothing tastes sweeter than success

E. *"Body Language"*, brings to light the significance of effective use of your body language for succeeding in the interviews. It also gives importance to the interviewer's body language during the interviews.

F. *"Interview Follow-up"*, deals with the follow-up of the interviews including the details of writing the thank-you letter, receiving the job offer, replying to a job offer and declining the offer.

Happy Reading!

SUBHASH JAGOTA

Before the Interview

Food for Thought

PREPARATION PAYS

Ashok was a final year student in one of the good management institute of India. Being a Mechanical Engineer and having a keen interest in automobiles, he wanted to get into the automobile industry, which he felt was an upcoming industry. He spent four months reading all he could about automobiles, the market in Europe, India and US; the market shares, the strengths and weaknesses of each brand; the problems of infrastructure, the best practices in the Automobile Industry etc. During his stay at the institute, he had gone for the in-company training to Escorts, he also went for plant visits to Hero Honda, attended seminars on automobiles and visited various auto exhibitions from time to time. Then he applied to the new automobile entrants in India.

Ashok was called for an interview by one of the company. He studied the balance sheet of the organisation, went through the web-site and the corporate brochures and became familiar with the organisation. During the interview he was very confident. He came out with flying colours. He was excited to receive the offer and readily accepted it. Good preparation had led to a predictable result!

The more you can sell yourself in the interview, the better are your chances of success

Before the Interview

When an employer is interviewing a potential employee he is looking for skills that an employee can apply on the job. He will also be trying to figure out his personality and how he will fit in with existing team in the organisation.

The key to succeed in an interview is preparation and it should include the following:

KNOW – YOURSELF

The first step should be a self-assessment of your strengths and weaknesses, which will help you know what you are most suited for and what actually you want. This will enable you to emphasise on your strong points so that you can do something to counteract the negative ones.

The key to success is
knowing yourself

Some questions which may be useful in self-assessment:

- What are your skills, abilities, and accomplishments? Be prepared to present your skills such as, communication skills, leadership and problem solving skills and relate your skills to the needs of the position and the organisation.
- What is your work style or personality trait? Explain how your work style and personality trait distinguishes you from other candidates.
- What are your expectations from the job that you are applying for? Decide whether you want job security, good working conditions, advancement opportunities, and family considerations etc.
- What are your weaknesses? In addition to identifying your strengths, you need to be aware of your weaknesses. In an interview always choose a weakness that you are

Gathering information
about the company beforehand
will certainly help you in making
a positive impact in the interview

striving to improve or a weakness that can also be a strength. For example, I am a perfectionist, which at times may bother my team members, but I feel that no product should be delivered to the customer until it is perfect since it is a direct reflection of the quality of our work.

Know – The Organisation

Find out everything you can about the organisation before the interview. This information will allow you to focus on your skills, experience, and interests in the interview that relate to the company. Employer research will also help you to anticipate the questions and fine tune your answers.

What information to gather

- **History and size of the organisation:** When was the organisation set-up, what is the total number of employees in the organisation, what are the various divisions that

Identify your talent
& be realistic of what you can do
for self as well as
organisational growth

the organisation is diversified into. How many plants does the organisation have – the locations of the plants and their areas of operations.

- **Products and services:** An overview of the products and services offered by the organisation and the areas it specialises in. What areas does the organisation plan to diversify into in the future?
- **Growth and earnings:** What is the position of the organisation in the market – the rate of growth of the organisation, the annual turnover of the organisation.
- **Career paths and training programmes:** What are the programmes provided for the development of the employees and the opportunities for their growth.
- **Geographic locations of the head office and divisions:** Where are the various offices, divisions and plants of the organisation located.

Good preparation
before the
interview leads to
predictable results

Where to gather the information from

- Browsing Internet to visit the organisation's website.
- Visiting the organisation in advance and going through the corporate brochures and annual reports.
- Talking to others in the organisation.
- Attending 'Career Festivals': These fairs and festivals are dedicated to bringing the community, employers, educators and students together to explore career pathways in the future and understanding the expectations of the industry. The students are given first-hand insights into the available career opportunities.

KNOW - POTENTIAL JOB

Don't make assumptions about the available position based upon the title. Two positions with identical titles may require very different skills and distinctly different duties. Try to know

Each individual should be accountable to pay cheque he gets

the job profile before the interview and understand the organisation chart. Armed with this information you will have a better sense of the strengths necessary to succeed in the position you are applying for.

Match yourself to the job

When you have made an initial assessment of your strengths and weaknesses and are clear about what the job requires then it is easier to recognise whether you are genuinely suited for the job or not.

Some questions to see how you match up to the job

- ❑ What does this job involve and what will be expected from me?
- ❑ Do I have the kind of experience they are looking for?

Your biodata, though brief,
should be complete in all respects

- ❑ What skills are they looking for and do I have those skills? If not, could I learn them?
- ❑ Does the job require a lot of travelling?
- ❑ How can I contribute to the growth and success of the organisation?
- ❑ Will the job fit in with my family commitments?

DRAFTING YOUR RESUME

Once you have done the self-assessment and matched yourself to the job, the next step is to draft your resume.

The first impression of a candidate lies in the style and content of his resume. One must make sure that it's properly worded, rightly formatted and free of grammatical errors.

Your resume is your personal representative and make a great first impression

The resume should be a one to two page, well articulated packaging of your skills, achievements and education, written in a manner that grabs the interviewer's attention. Its main purpose is to win in the interview. It should be customised for a particular company and the job profile in mind. Hence, it should be original and geared towards a specific career goal.

The language should be very objective. Specific details pertaining to present tenure, job title and the field in which you wish to work, however, should definitely be included.

While giving the references, make sure that you brief them adequately before the interviewer calls them for cross-reference. Also, if you are casually dropping names in the interview make sure you mention those who will sing your praise.

Going for the Interview

Food for Thought

PREPARE FOR CONTINGENCIES

Rahul had started out from Shalimar Bagh, for an interview at Nehru Place. He was looking for the position of a Management Trainee at the entry level in a large conglomerate.

He had allotted about an hour for the journey, which seemed ample. He thought that he would get off the bus at Nehru Place itself and go to the respective office. When he actually got there, he realised that the interview was scheduled to be in the other branch office which was at Connaught Place, about 30 minutes from there. He rushed out and could not find a taxi for about 20 minutes. Then he got one and reached the office half an hour after the scheduled time.

Rahul went through the interview and did very well during the interview, but was not selected. *He always wondered whether it was the 'half an hour late' that changed his destiny!*

Find out in advance how to get to the interview venue.

It won't do you any good to get lost

Going for the Interview

You have an interview appointment. While going for an interview, your immediate concern is how to make yourself the candidate who is most likely to succeed.

Here are some tips you should take into consideration while going for the interview:

PUNCTUALITY

The first step towards success is to arrive for your interview about 15 or 20 minutes early, leave time for contigencies – breakdown of the car, missing the bus etc. Punctuality always

One should not carry a helmet, big briefcase etc., along with him to the interviewers room gives a good impression and it helps you remain calm and confident, which is very important while appearing for an interview. Knowledge of the time it takes to reach the interview venue, the route and the location, will give you confidence, which will show through in the interview. If you are late you may irritate the interviewer or lose your appointment altogether. Make sure you have the correct address. Confirm the location of the interview by telephone or any other media and find out the best means of getting there.

WHAT TO TAKE TO THE INTERVIEW

There are some essential things you will want to take along with you when you go for a job interview but avoid taking too many things along with you. If it is raining or likely to rain, it is a good precaution to be armed with an umbrella or a raincoat but you should certainly not take it to the interviewer's room.

You will never get a second chance to make a good first impression

Similarly, you should not carry a helmet, big briefcase etc. along with you to the interviewer's room.

If you are Late

If, in spite of all your planning, you find you are going to be late, try to inform the office so that the interview can be rescheduled and apologise in a straightforward way with a brief reason. A lengthy excuse always sounds less convincing.

Being Polite to Everyone you Meet

Whether you are late or early, it is wise to be polite and pleasant to everyone you come in contact with. Remember it is not enough to be good to the interviewer only but also to all those who come in contact with you before or after the interview. The nicer you are to people, the more they will help you to relax.

It's always better to have a checklist before going for an interview

Interview checklist	✓ Or ×
Interview call letter	
Original testimonials along with xerox copies so that the same can be offered when required	
Extra copy of the application you had sent against the advertisement	
Two recent passport size photographs, contact person & the telephone number of the office where you are going to attend the interview	
In case you are in employment, present pay-slip from the employer	
Visiting card & personal letter head if you have got one	
Plain paper, pins, stapler, pen or a pocket diary	
Pocket calendar & calculator	
Reading material in case you are required to spend extra time before the interview start	

Dress for Success

Food for Thought

DRESSING FOR THE OCCASION

Priya was appearing before the interview panel for the post of an 'Executive Assistant' in a large conglomerate. She managed to impress the members on the panel with her intelligence, excellent communication skills, job knowledge and pleasing personality. Everyone found her to be the right candidate for the position. Nevertheless, she could not make it.

The only thing that acted as an obstruction in her selection was her overall appearance. She was dressed informally, wearing a pair of jeans and a T-shirt. Her job would require her to organise meetings and interact with senior executives. Her style of dressing-up didn't match to the job profile for which she was being interviewed. Basically, besides other things, **your appearance really makes a lot of difference.**

Always dress smartly & comfortably – getting it right will make you feel more confident & calm

Dress for Success

You will never get a second chance to make a good first impression

This is very true for the interview also. Research shows that the people form 90% of their opinion about you within a minute and a half of meeting you. Your appearance, therefore, contributes to a great extent in making a positive impact in the interview.

Dress for Success

It is very important for the potential candidate to ensure that he/she wears appropriate clothes for the occasion. Though selection of a candidate will not be determined by the dress alone, nevertheless, it creates a first impression about the

It is imperative for
all managers to understand
the behavioural intricacies of different
working cultures, especially taking into view
the body language, postures, customs
and certain work ethics, specific
to the working culture.

candidate. If the first impression is poor because of inappropriate and careless attire, there are chances that the candidate may be rejected.

It may be appropriate to wear the dress as per the culture and norms in the organisation. However, the best thing to do is to use your own judgement and wear whatever looks professional and comfortable to you. So create a situation that will make the potential employer want to buy the product i.e. you. When the outfit is appropriate, the interviewer can concentrate on the other factors such as your caliber, experience and personality.

If the interviewer is dressed casually and you formally, it may not reflect negatively on you, but if she is dressed formally and you are in your casuals, it can surely have a negative impact on the interviewer.

Your appearance should reflect well on you, right from your hairstyle to your shoes

The following should be kept in mind while choosing a dress for the interview:

AVOID EXTREMES

There are a lot of things, which can be said about appearance, however, the most important is that you should avoid extremes and wear something, which you feel comfortable in. Some tips can be:

Clothing

- Conservative and neat
- Neutrality is important
- Avoid coloured clothes
- Wear black or dark shoes and ensure that they are properly polished
- Combine personal style with good taste

- Wear something that makes you feel terrific and is comfortable
- Use simple accessories like simple jewellery, watches, ties etc.

Grooming

- Hair and make up should be neat and not attract attention
- Scents, perfumes and aftershaves should be subdued... don't overdue it
- Hand and nails must be manicured

The above points may appear trivial but are very important in your selection.

Have a Balanced Approach:

What to Say, What Not to Say

Food for Thought

HAVE A BALANCED APPROACH

Vishal was appearing before the interview panel for the post of an Assistant Manager. Talking about his background, Vishal told the panel about his academic and professional achievements. The panel was really impressed with the qualifications and the significant contributions made by him in his present organisation. At the end of the interview when Vishal was asked about the reason for wanting to leave his present job, he started complaining about his present employer by saying that "My current employer does not know how to treat people, he is unfair and terrible to work with

This statement made a negative impact on the panel. The panel felt that no doubt Vishal had all the skills required for the job but he might be having some attitudinal problems and might face the same problems in their organisation. Considering all the facts, the panel declared Vishal as unsuitable for the post.

An interview is a focussed, goal-oriented exchange of information between two or more people

Have a Balanced Approach:

What to Say, What Not to Say

Interview is basically a conversation to find out how well two sides of a potential deal might suit one another. The employer is offering money and status. You are offering your time and expertise. In an interview you should not parade all your negative traits in front of the interviewer. However, what you say should be the truth.

BE POSITIVE AND ENTHUSIASTIC

Think positive and be enthusiastic. Your tone of voice should show enthusiasm. If you are able to liven up the discussion, it

People ask you to be critical of them but they only want praise will create a good impression and help you to relax. Don't sound too timid or tough because these are often seen as signs of weakness.

Listen Carefully to the Questions

You must make a positive effort to listen to the interviewer and answer the questions, which the interviewer actually puts across to you. Make sure that you understand what has been asked.

Handling Silence in the Interview

A moment of silence gives you the opportunity to elaborate on some of your skills that are related to the position, but which have not yet been addressed in the interviewer's questions. Plan in advance how you want to handle silent moments in the interview.

The overall success of any individual depends not just on technical skills but also on soft skills and behaviour

Develop your own uniqueness/worth

Keep your Answers Informative but not Too Long

Try not to give '*one – word answers*' in 'Yes' or 'No'. At the same time don't be too detailed in what you say. *Keep your answers brief and concise while still imparting all the relevant information.* By, talking too much by you may end up revealing more than you had intended.

Don't Talk About Religion / Politics

Don't talk about politics or religion unless you are sure that the interviewer will agree with your viewpoint, as you may not know the viewpoints of the interviewer.

Practice Out Loud

Practice your answers loudly. It will show your positive attitude and enthusiasm, which will take you through the interview.

Have an edge over other through influencing skills

THINK ABOUT WHAT YOU SAY

Tell the interviewer which parts of the job really attracts you and why for example, if you are saying that you are 'interested in this post because it is a challenge' without any explanation of what the challenge is, forget it!

THINK ABOUT QUESTIONS IN ADVANCE

No one can predict the exact questions that an interviewer will ask, but you can rehearse your resume and get a good idea of a few questions that the employer is likely to ask. Be sure that all the questions an interviewer asks are with a reason, although some may seem to be irrelevant and some unnecessarily personal. So, to prepare, think about how you would answer the following questions:

Self-analysis of your
strengths
& weaknesses will help you
move one step ahead towards success

Self-knowledge is the beginning
of self improvement

SAMPLE INTERVIEW QUESTIONS

1. How would you describe your home background?

   Tip: Try to pick out the aspects of your background, which make you especially suitable for the job you have applied for. Never include the negative aspects of your home background. Points to stress include stability, an encouraging and positive attitude to education, parents or relatives who have been involved in similar work, and an enthusiastic attitude to hard work.

2. What is your greatest strength?

   Tip: This is a great question to show your uniqueness. If as suggested you have done some background work on self-analysis then you will be in a good position to answer this.

   Technical skills are necessary but attitudinal skills, matter most in the journey to success. Interviewers look for

Now a days interviewers not only see the skills required, but also give great emphasis on a positive attitude positive attitude, fire of enthusiasm, ability and keenness to learn, good team players, good interpersonal skills so as to interact with clients effectively, ability to think BIG and grow in the organisation. Candidates who are willing to go anywhere across the globe and work in different environments have competitive edge over others.

Be prepared with some examples as the interviewer will not accept whatever you say at its face value and will cross check on you.

3. What is your greatest weakness?

Tip: Once again the key to this is to be positive. Do not say, 'I don't have any weakness'. On the other hand, if you categorise all your weaknesses for the interviewer you will surely show yourself as unsuitable for the job.

Having the certificate is important, but more important is to develop your personality and uniqueness

Always choose a weakness that you are striving to improve or a weakness that can also be a strength.

4. Why did you study (xxx) subjects at school / college?

   Tip: Make your answer a constructive one. You could bring up the point that how learning certain subjects has given you an edge over others or helped you in attaining extra skills. Never say you do not know why you have picked any particular subject, or that your parents decided for you, as this will show that you lack the ability to make decisions on your own.

5. Why do you want to work for this company?

   Tip: The interviewer is looking for a positive and enthusiastic approach towards the company. If, as suggested, you have done some background work on the

No matter where you work, you are not an employee, you are in business with your employer. Nobody owes your career, you are its sole proprietor company, you will be in a good position to say what you really like about it, why you think it has a reputation as a good employer, why this jobs suits you ideally.

6. If you and all the other potential employees had the same background in education and experience what would make the interviewer hire you over the others?

   Tip: Use employability skills. The employer wants to know that you are the best potential employee. (Ex. I know how an organisation such as yours works. I understand the right procedures and paths to follow to get the work accomplished efficiently and professionally. I am also a team player who can work well with all people and use their unique personalities to get the best results.)

7. Tell me about a situation where something went very wrong or you failed?

Many a times the difference between accomplishment and failure is your attitude

Tip: Employers want to see that you can handle a bad situation and turn it around into a positive situation. Be prepared to provide examples of occasions when results were different than expected. Remember that your skills in handling failure as well as success will be probed in the interview.

8. Why are you leaving your current position?

   Tip: The key is to be positive. The interviewer is trying to find out if you left your last job for reasons, which could pose similar problems, if you came to work in the new job. Employers are looking for employees with positive attitudes even if they have worked in bad situations. Complaining about your past employer will not win over a new employer. (e.g. "I am looking for a company that will give me the opportunity for better personal growth." This is much better then saying "My

What you want to be is more important than what you are

current employer does not know how to treat people, he is unfair and terrible to work with"). If you want to leave because you are bored, say that you have outgrown the job, or something similar. Another acceptable reason is the relocation of your company and your not wanting to go to a new place. Remember not to use this explanation if your potential employer requires mobility or the job you are applying for requires travelling.

If you cite the reason for leaving as a career change, make sure that interviewer realises that you are not going to change your mind again and that you are settled now. Give clear reasons as to why that change was beneficial and indicate that you are a quick learner.

9. What did you do in your last job?

Tip: Keep answers informative but not too long. Here the interviewer is looking for two things. First, how far the

Make yourself aware of benchmark practices in your field of work skills and experience acquired and used in your last job match up to those necessary to the new job. Second, how successful is your last job, so that he can gauge the potential you have. So, do not simply a list out the work you have been doing, but show how the experience you have gained in other job has directly fitted you to do the new one.

10. Be Prepared for Technical Questions

    Tip: If you are working in a technical field you should do your homework before the interview so that you are prepared for detailed questions. But be sure that in the interview you communicate technical information simply, without using jargons and without assuming that your interviewer is an expert on the subject. If you are not sure that the interviewer is an expert, prefix your statements with "as you are aware of" or "as you know".

If you don't know the answer, be honest & say so

For example, in many cases, the HRD Manager conducts the first interview and he may not be a technical person.

11. The awkward or unexpected question

Every one gets caught now and then with a totally unexpected question. If you don't know the answer, be honest and say so.

Body Language: Says it All!

Food for Thought

THE FIRST IMPRESSION

"Did you notice Siddharth's gestures while answering?" The General Manager asked the Manager. He was constantly fiddling with his ring and tapping his feet. Also while answering, he could not make an eye contact. This shows his nervousness and lack of confidence.

In the first three minutes of observing him, the GM had made up his mind that he would not recruit this person. He was not impressed with Siddharth's body movements. Siddharth had knowledge about many subjects and his past record revealed that he had been successful throughout his academic life. But at that moment his body language seemed to overshadow his achievements, academic excellence etc. As a result, Siddharth was not selected.

The way you speak is
as important as what you speak...

Body Language: Says it All!

Do you have a body movement, which you use when nervous or excited? It could be rubbing your ear or palm when nervous. It could be holding your chin when thinking deeply. These movements are basically involuntary. They are habits that are acquired by each individual over time, but they are consistent and can be read by others to reveal underlying feelings.

During an interview, non-verbal communication carries ever-lasting impressions. People tend to believe actions more than words. What we do with our hands while speaking, how we express ourselves, and whether we make eye contact, how

His actions spoke so loudly, I couldn't hear what he said

we sit, stand and move all are important and form a few elements of the body language. Our bodies speak and say a lot about who we are and how we feel about ourselves. Here is a quick refresher on body language before any important meeting. These are tips for successful, unobtrusive, non-verbal communication...

- ❑ **POSTURE:** Carrying yourself well as you walk into the interview room will create an initial positive impression with your interviewer and indicate confidence. So stand and walk with your head erect and shoulders back, and keep your style of walking confident. During the interview, sitting up in your chair and leaning forward tend to indicate your interest. Put your arms slightly in front of you. A woman should place her handbag on the floor next to her to avoid the possibility of sitting defensively crouched over it on her lap.

People tend to believe actions more than words!

- **HANDS:** One of the most frequently observed but least understood cues are the hand movements. Some movement of hands while talking is natural, but be sure they're not swinging about wildly. Keep your hand gestures to a minimum. Also be sure to keep your hands visible at all times, as not doing so can send a subliminal message that you are not trustworthy.

- **HANDSHAKE:** Shaking hands well is an art. Everyone should receive a firm but not bone-crushing handshake. A firm handshake during the introduction can show confidence and assertiveness. Also be sure not to pump the other person's hand and arm too vigorously or for too long. Quick, one or two pumps will suffice. And use only one hand: the two-handed shake reminds one of the receiving line at occasions.

- **FACIAL EXPRESSIONS:** Facial expressions continually change during interaction and are monitored constantly

Of all the things you wear, your expression is the most important

by the interviewer. During the interview if you want to give the impression of being an energetic and reliable person, then you must have a pleasant expression and smile on your face. A face that looks relaxed gives the impression that you are not only a pleasant person to deal with, but a confident one, too. A face with tensed jaw, nervous twitches or stern expression does not impress anyone. So do not hesitate to smile in the interview when appropriate. In general, be sure your facial expression matches with what you are saying. For e.g., if you are discussing a serious issue, a smile would be inappropriate.

- **EYE CONTACT:** Eye contact is a direct and powerful form of non – verbal communication. The frequency of contact may suggest either interest or boredom. So it is very important to maintain good eye contact. The best way is to have a balanced look in the eyes of interviewer without

Attitudes are mirrors of the mind, they reflect thinking

staring them down. Friendly, attentive eye contact conveys sincerity, interest and confidence. To do so, concentrate on making eye contacts most of the time. If you have more than one interviewer, include each one in your answers by moving your eyes from one to other.

- **TONE OF VOICE:** Speak in a clear, well-modulated, audible voice. Many people tend to show their nervousness by talking rapidly. Check your voice tone, inflection, and volume during the interview. Remember that your voice is a primary instrument of communication.

- **OTHER GESTURES:** Watch out for such unnecessary and unprofessional gestures as tapping your foot, fiddling with your watch, ring or other jewellery, twirling your hair and drumming your fingers on the chair arm or desk. Not only are these movements distracting, but they imply that you are nervous, impatient or bored.

A good way to check that you are giving the right amount of information is to observe the interviewers' body language

Expressing yourself clearly & concisely is a key element in an effective interview

THE INTERVIEWERS' BODY LANGUAGE

Pay attention to the interviewers' body language. Are they paying attention to you? Are they turning towards you, leaning forward, nodding and smiling? If so, great! You are on the right track with your responses to their questions.

Are they turning away from you, not making eye contact? Shuffling papers? Do they have a posture, which is slumped away from you? Are their arms crossed in front of them? If so, it is time to re-group as your responses to their questions may be off track. Ask them to rephrase the question. Are they interested in a particular aspect of your response?

Think in advance how you want to respond if their body language shows that you are on the wrong track.

By inculcating the above points in your body expressions, you can make your communication more effective.

A little nervousness is a good thing but too much of it can ruin the interview

A FEW USEFUL TIPS

- Be positive about yourself. You have been invited to an interview because you are a good candidate. The interviewer has seen your application and must have been impressed.
- Remain calm, be enthusiastic about the job and be realistic about your strengths and weaknesses. The worst that can happen is, you won't get the job.
- Take a deep breath, calm yourself and enter the interview room slowly and soberly. Be ready to listen to the interviewer who will initiate the conversation.
- Walk over to the chair, shake hands if the interviewer offers his hand first.
- If you are worried then your hands will be sweating because of anxiety and nervousness. You shouldn't normally initiate the handshake but should be ready to

Boost your self-confidence & improve your self-image for achieving higher results

respond. Your handshake should be firm, not gripping or domineering. It is supposed to be a gesture of friendliness.

- Don't hold the interviewer's hand for too long, smile at the interviewer and look at him in the eyes as you shake hands. Don't shake hands looking downwards.
- When you sit down, don't slouch and try not to freeze into one position. Breathe.
- Try to eliminate nervous gestures such as toe tapping, hair pulling, scratching, fidgeting with props, etc.
- The interviewer will be doing his best to put you at ease. Most candidates look a bit nervous - interviewers are very used to this. So they start with some question regarding the weather or your journey to the office etc. Don't take these questions very seriously. The interviewer will want to hear your answers in good spoken English. You must be clear and audible.

The difference between success and the failure is your attitude towards the life

- Don't put your hands over your mouth as you speak or you will not be heard as easily and will appear more nervous. The interviewers want to hear simple answers, which are not too long and show a good grasp of the facts. Talking too much will probably irritate the interviewer.

- Your answers should be backed by examples. Speak slowly and deliberately, pause for a few seconds during answering, this will also help you relax.

- It is important to show a sense of humor as this will reflect your positive attitude. Observe whether the interviewer is listening. If not, vary the pace of your speech, or stop for a moment.

- Try to use silence to the best of your advantage by mentioning your strengths as discussed earlier.

Candidates Must be Prepared to Ask Questions Too

Candidates Must be Prepared to Ask Questions Too

Job interviews allow both the employer and the candidate to raise questions and evaluate each other so that both can make a better employment decision.

The candidate should be actively involved in the interview process. He should take into account that the interviewer will be expecting questions related to the company and job. Therefore, before an interview, the candidate should prepare some questions to ask during the pre-interview stage and the interview stage. A candidate should only ask questions on

An interview is a two-way process, the active involvement of both parties is necessary relevant topics, which are meaningful and require clarifications. The kind of questions that the candidate asks should also indicate his understanding about the different issues related to responsibilities.

Here is list of questions, which may suggest the kinds of things you can ask about.

Pre-Interview Questions:

- ❑ Ask for the name of the person who is speaking to you on the phone (receptionist, interviewer, head of the company/ department, etc.).
- ❑ Who will be interviewing me?

Candidates may ask any of the following questions:

- ❑ What will be the job profile of the position?
- ❑ Possibilities for relocation and travel

In an interview, communicate what you can contribute for the success of the organisation

- ❑ Training programmes - initial and future
- ❑ Career paths and opportunities for advancement
- ❑ Performance reviews/evaluations
- ❑ Organisational structure - departmental structure
- ❑ Products, services, plans for the future

Ask the following questions tactfully, early in an interview to assess what an interviewer is looking for, so that you are able to formulate your responses accordingly.

- ❑ The major short and long-term goals of the organisation
- ❑ Organisation's structure and management style
- ❑ Expectations from the position
- ❑ Type of people employed by the organisation
- ❑ The values of the organisation

Interview Follow-up

Interview Follow-up

ANALYSE YOUR INTERVIEW PERFORMANCE

After the interview is over, you should review your performance as soon as possible, before the impressions and memories fade. Every interview can be a useful and constructive experience and doing a proper follow-up will help you to achieve the most of it, even if you are not successful in getting the job. As soon as you arrive home, prepare a checklist and go through it to see how you have performed. When you see how you have marked it, think about the answers you gave and pinpoint the answers which were not satisfactory.

Don't appear too eager at the end of the interview. Leave with a pleasant smile on your face

Questions you should rethink or practice:

- ❑ About the previous job specially the achievements
- ❑ Reason for leaving the last job
- ❑ Academic achievements
- ❑ Future plans

Before the next interview get to work on the weaknesses identified by you in the checklist. If the main problem is how to present yourself, try to find someone who will practice mock interviews with you.

"Rather than getting ahead of others
it more important to get ahead
of ourself and break our self
record for success.

Use each failure as feedback for constant progress towards your success

Post Interview Checklist	
1.	Was I punctual for the interview?
2.	Was my dress appropriate?
3.	Was I confident while entering the interview room?
4.	Was my posture correct?
5.	Was I able to control nervousness during the interview?
6.	Did I listen attentively?
7.	Was I able to answer questions according to the job applied?
8.	Were my qualifications appreciated by the interviewer?
9.	Did I pointout my special strengths, which can be utilised in the job?
10.	Was I able to cope with questions about my weaknesses?
11.	Did I demonstrate how I was best suited to the job?
12.	Have I given appropriate references?
13.	Was I able to ask appropriate questions?
14.	Did I look at the interviewer while talking and maintain eye contact?
15.	Was my handshake appropriate at the end of the interview?

Writing a 'Thank You letter'
shows that you are courteous &
makes you stand out among other candidates

INTERVIEW FOLLOW-UP: WHAT IT IS & WHY IT'S NEEDED

Follow-up basically means that within one to two days of your interview, you prepare and send a personal note of thanks to those who interviewed you. Writing a follow - up indicates that you are courteous, knowledgeable about the job and still interested in the position. The basic points to are:

- ❑ Thank them for calling you for the interview.
- ❑ Thank them for their time and consideration
- ❑ Highlight any unique strength which is relevant to the position
- ❑ Indicate that you look forward to hearing from them.

Sending a thank you letter is an important step in the interviewing process. Not only is it proper etiquette, but it makes you stand out among those candidates who may not have sent a letter.

SAMPLE OF A JOB ACCEPTANCE LETTER

1st January 2001

Dear Mr. / Ms. ________________

Thank you for your job offer dated ___________, which I am happy to accept.

I confirm I will start work on January 2001 at 9.30 a.m.

Looking forward to joining your organisation.

Yours sincerely

Rajesh Malhotra

THANK YOU LETTER OUTLINE

Your Street Address
City, State, Zip Code

Employer's Name, Title
Company/Organisation
Dear ___________:

INTRODUCTION includes:

- ❑ Day of your interview
- ❑ Position for which you were interviewed
- ❑ Statement of appreciation for the interview
- ❑ Express continued interest in the position and the company

MAIN BODY (usually one or two small paragraphs) includes:

- ❑ Reaffirm your most valuable skills and qualifications and how you expect to contribute to the company
- ❑ Include any information you forgot to mention in the interview. Be brief.

CLOSING includes:

- ❑ Statement of appreciation
- ❑ Comment regarding future contact with the employer

Sincerely,

Your Name and Signature

Burning desire to win

is first step towards success

Rather than getting ahead of

others it more is important to get ahead

of ourself and break our self

record for success

Even though you may not be offered the job, the impression made on the interviewer is usually very positive and can lead to employment in the same organisation at a later date. It is worth the time and effort involved.

COPING WITH REJECTION

An important part of interview follow - up is coping with possible rejection. Usually many more people apply for a job than those who can be successful. You shouldn't take rejection too personally in these circumstances. The important thing is to approach each interview as a totally separate entity. Do not carry the feeling of rejection from one situation to the next. If you do so you will approach the next interview with the wrong frame of mind and it will make you less effective.

Be not afraid of growing slowly, be afraid only of standing still

Receiving a Job Offer

1. A job offer may be made in person or by phone followed up by a letter. Do not consider an offer "bona fide" until it is confirmed in writing.
2. The employer will indicate salary, benefits, job title, location, perhaps a starting date (or will ask you for a starting date), and perhaps a deadline for your reply.

Replying to a Job Offer

1. Remember that responding to a job offer is an "art" and requires sensitive negotiation. You need to consider the needs of the employer, the current job market, your work preferences and values, and your willingness to take risks.
2. Always acknowledge a job offer immediately, generally in writing.
3. If the employer does not specify a deadline for your acceptance and if you do not want to accept the offer immediately, acknowledge the offer and express your

Remember that responding to a job offer is an 'art' & requires sensitive negotiation interest in the position. Then ask how soon they need a decision or mention your time - frame.

4. In accepting an offer, write a letter of acceptance, restating the salary, starting date, and where to report to work. It's also a good idea to call.

5. If you are undecided about the position, take some time to think about it.

6. It is permissible to ask for more time, especially if you are given only a short time to consider an offer. You should specify the amount of time you would like. Be aware that there is some risk involved here.

Declining an Offer

1. Reply as soon as possible in writing.

2. Indicate why you are declining if you can do so tactfully and constructively. You may just say that you have accepted a position with another organisation or you may indicate its name.

SELECTED

3. End with an appropriate statement to keep the door open for some possible future contact.

Things that the candidate must know before he starts the new job include:

- Date on which the new job begins
- The starting salary
- Date on which the first salary increase will be considered
- Whether the offer is subject to the approval of satisfactory references, medical reports, provisions of proof of qualifications, work permits
- Details of relocation arrangements
- Details of all fringe benefits like company car, commission or bonus scheme
- Contract of employment

Little Things which Make a Big Difference

Little Things which Make a Big Difference

Things to be kept in mind while going for an interview

- Be on time or a little early to avoid any anxiety
- Be relaxed but confident during the interview
- Dress appropriately- formals are the best choice
- Use an attentive posture and watch your non-verbal behavior
- Express your strengths and accomplishments assertively

Conquer your fears and anxiety and motivate yourself to success

- Express your strengths and accomplishments assertively.
- Prepare interview questions in advance - write down some points and practice aloud.
- Give concrete examples in support of your points.
- Speak in a confident voice; be enthusiastic.
- Take time to formulate your answers before you speak.
- Eye contact is critical – especially when making your key points, but don't stare.
- Make a thorough study of the Company and the job.
- Customise your skills according to the employer's needs.
- Control your personal signs of nervousness such as finger tapping, leg swinging, fidgeting, etc.
- Follow-up the interview; send a thank you letter within 24 hours of the interview.

Boost your self-confidence
& improve your self-image

Things to be avoided

- Do not evade questions or be afraid to ask questions
- Do not go into too much detail, 60 seconds responses are appropriate. Don't race through your answer- take your time.
- Don't bring your social life into the interview, volunteer personal information especially values, associations and bad experiences.
- Avoid speaking negatively about your previous employer
- Don't make hasty or sweeping generalisations
- Avoid answering in simple "YES" or "NO" responses. Give responses with descriptive examples and try to paint a visual picture for the employer.
- Don't use technical jargons. However, if a member of panel continues to probe you in any technical field you can use technical expressions

Few Words of Wisdom from Experts

While interviewing candidates, earlier I used to pay much attention to technical skills but now I feel it is attitudinal skills, which matters the most in the journey to success

Interviewers try to look for values, integrity, motivation & commitment in candidates. They want someone who will work hard in return for what the company gives

Interviewing Skills

By: Mr. R K Kapila

Director & Facilitator, Organisation Development Solutions

(Ex-GM – Training & Development, Modi Xerox)

"Skills can always be developed
but Values, which come from the family &
environment do not change"

When I interview candidates I always give much attention and weightage to the following characteristics:

- **Core values:** It is very important for candidates to have core values, which come from the family and environment. Unless these values are strong, a person can't perform to a high level. Core values are deep-rooted traits that summarise a person's integrity, honesty, responsibility, openness, and fairness in dealing with others.

Communication is the
vehicle for all other skills

- **Responsiveness / Commitment:** A burning desire and commitment to achieve is the starting point of all accomplishments. "Total commitment is paramount to reaching the ultimate in performance." A candidate should exhibit commitment towards team members, thereby, inculcating a sense of belongingness. He should respect the credibility and integrity of everyone in the company.
- **Respecting human values:** In today's competitive world managers need to transact outside their own regions and religion. Empathy i.e., being able to "put yourself in the other person shoes" is a key trait of leaders today. Therefore one should respect others, their values and feelings
- **Positive attitude is everything**: Through proper training and seminars, knowledge & skills can be developed but attitude is something, which remains the same and directly affects the working of person.

Skills can always be developed but Values, which come from the family & environment do not change

- **Communication and presentation skills:** Success of a person will depend upon how effectively he can put his ideas across to those whom he works with, thereby, persuading others to work in the direction of the achievement of goals of the organisation.

The quality and speed of output that the group produces, depends upon the quality of communication. Communication can enable an organisation to display a significant increase in productivity through better team building, delegation, employee motivation and information sharing.

Between average & high performing organisations, it is the people who make the difference

Interviewing Skills

By: Mr. D K Bakshi

GM - HR, Luxor Writing Instruments Ltd. (LWIL)

In Luxor the selection of candidates has always been a very serious matter. Between average and high performing organisations, it is the people who make the difference. So some of the qualities we are looking for in the candidates are:

- **Emotional stability:** Today's working environment requires long working hours and achieving targets in the specified time periods, therefore, the candidate must be able to tolerate stress and perform efficiently. He should be able to take decisions with the minimum resources available to him and shouldn't take decisions in haste.

Select individuals who have the potential to grow & assume higher responsibilities to inspire others

- **Self-Motivation:** Motivation drives all human actions. It is the source of energy. As an interviewer I look for individuals who are self-motivated and have the potential and drive to reach at the top.

- **Enthusiasm:** Candidates should display enthusiasm by being active, expressive and energetic. They should be optimistic and open to change. We would like to select enthusiastic team members who have the ability to satisfy customer needs and provide customer delight. We strongly feel that only satisfied employees can do so.

- **Knowledge of subject on which you are working:** It is a known fact that "Knowledge is the currency of this millennium." While interviewing we see that the candidate has full knowledge of his subject / industry and also know what is going on in other industries.

We would like to select enthusiastic team members who have the ability to satisfy customer needs & provide customer delight. We strongly feel that only satisfied employees can do so

- **Potential to Grow:** Candidates should strive to realise their full potential towards the path of success.
- **Passion:** Candidates should have the passion to pave the way for rapid growth through continuous improvement by innovation and create a significant competitive edge, which is comparable to world standards.

What you have already achieved is not as important as having qualities that will take you forward

Interviewing Skills

By: Mr. K K Ahuja

Executive Director – HR,

Gujarat Heavy Industries Ltd

Recruiting In The New Century

"The definition of a candidate's profile is changing", said Mr. Ahuja. "Earlier, education and experience used to be the criteria for selection. Now there is a rising emphasis on behavioral characteristics of the candidates. What you have already achieved is not as important as having qualities that will take you forward.

As an individual one should have talent i.e., capability to create value that is recognised and rewarded by primary stakeholders – owners, managers and customers. In the present scenario

Select individuals who can deliver results & work efficiently in teams to make a valuable contribution to the company the job usually requires some degree of pro-activity, creativity, initiative, speed and commitment towards teamwork. So I want to select individuals who deliver results and work efficiently in teams to make a valued contribution to the company."

The fresher, besides being aggressive, should also be a good team player

Interviewing Skills

By: Mr. G P S Chandel

GM - HR, Seimens India Ltd.

It's EQ that matters

I do not have any particular preference when it comes to A & B grade engineering and management institutes but I stress on personality attributes in the selection process. I look for a mindset which is open, positive, receptive and ready to accept difficult tasks, right attitude, emotional ability and an effective thinking process.

IQ is, no doubt, important but basic EQ (Emotional Quotient) is more important. Only an emotional stable person can meet the challenges of the future. Today, the route to growth for any company is through innovation and change management. This necessitates building flexibility, creativity and risk taking abilities.

The fresher, besides being aggressive, should also be a good team player.

The candidates with a killing instinct energy, a desire to excel and a flexible approach are chosen in Samsung

We view our employees, not merely as functional specialists, but as an interface between the market and the company

CAREERS AT SAMSUNG - INDIA*

By: Mr. S S Lee

Managing Director, Samsung – India

Samsung – India believes in training and moulding people to enable them to give their optimum. A killing instinct energy, a desire to excel and a flexible approach are the attributes looked for at the entry level. At the middle level, commitment and dedication are sought. People with drive and leadership qualities, besides a flexible approach ideally fit the bill. For top management, traits like leadership and vision, ability to motivate a team, macro-level thinking etc. count the most.

The success of Samsung – India is the result of the Human Management Philosophy that it follows: The organisation moves the world and the people move the organisation.

* Article published in "HT Career" 19th July, 2001.

Interviewer looks for the candidate who can contribute in terms of value addition to the job and the organisation

SUCCEEDING IN THE INTERVIEW

By: Mr. K K SINGH,

Chief Manager - HR, ESCORTS LTD.

There are no ideal jobs and no ideal candidates. There are only the *"Best Fits"* and the interview is only a process of finding that *"Best Fit"*. The interviewer just looks for this Best Fit and tries to find out the most suitable candidate for his requirements.

Being the Best Fit and the most suitable candidate is not that easy in this competitive world where people are in queue for the same position. *The most important aspect the interviewer looks in his 'Right Choice' is what the candidate can contribute in terms of Value Addition to the job and the organisation.*

The organisation needs only those people who can easily become a part of the system and contribute towards the success of the organisation. Functional skills, job knowledge or core competencies are the basic requirements of any job. There are

Be relaxed, take care of your body language and manage your personality reflections in the best possible way to get the job other desirable characteristics and qualities, which govern the suitability, adaptability and success of any candidate for the prospective job. Some of these characteristics and qualities the interviewer may look for in the new entrant can be like the following:

- Professional awareness in terms of domestic and global industry, market and economic scenario.
- Flexibility to adopt change in terms of location i.e. being ready to be located anywhere in their operating territory.
- Team spirit, interpersonal and communication skills in terms of speaking, listening, presentation, convincing etc.
- Achievement orientation and knowledge of the past achievements, both personal and professional.
- Self-awareness in terms of strengths and weaknesses.
- Inclination towards continuous improvement and progress.

Attitudinal skills and flexibility to adopt change matter the most in the journey to success

- ❑ Control over body language during the interview.
- ❑ Personal grooming, physical fitness and cheerful appearance.

Managing so many personality reflections effectively as well as impressing the interviewer in just 10-15 minutes seems to be really difficult. But if you want to get the job then there is no other choice but to make a impressive presentation.

Facing the interview definitely needs a systematic approach and comprehensive preparation for the event so as to impress the interviewer and clinch the job. It starts with creating the first impression with the feeling of *"You don't get a second chance to create a good first impression."* Be relaxed and take care of your body language and manage your personality reflections – physical, mental, and emotional in the best possible professional way and be the job winner.

Select individuals who think independently, have the courage to act on their own ideas & are self-directed

MAKE YOURSELF JOB FRIENDLY*

By: Mr. Subhash Jagota,

Executive Director - HR, Punj Lloyd Limited

Selecting the right people for employment plays an important role in determining an organisation's path toward success. Today corporate houses are looking for innovative ways of selecting people; some of them are as follows:

- In the past more emphasis has been given on technical skills but with the fast changing environment, more emphasis is given to attitudinal skills. Technical skills are necessary but it is attitudinal skills, which matter most in the journey to success. Today organisations are looking for candidates who have positive attitude, fire of enthusiasm, ability and keenness to learn, good team

* Article published in "The Indian Express" March 3, 2001

A burning desire is the starting point of all accomplishments. Just like a small fire cannot give much heat, a weak desire cannot produce results skills, ability to think BIG and grow in the organisation. Preference is given to the candidates who are willing to go anywhere across the globe and work in different environments. Besides the above-mentioned attributes they should also have good interpersonal skills so that they can interact with clients effectively.

- Organisations wish to recruit those candidates who are willing to act as self-starters and have the right attitude towards life. Individuals who have the potential to grow and assume higher responsibility in the organisation are always the preferred candidates. Organisations are looking for people who can fit into the company's vision, mission and values. Only those candidates should be recruited who can adjust with the company's values and culture and those who can contribute to strengthen the agreed upon values.

Collecting certificates is important but what is more important is developing personality & uniqueness

- Organisations are looking for entrepreneurs (entrepreneurs within the organisations) who can take risk, develop their network and deliver value to the organisation. Candidates should try to have contacts and develop a network in industry so as to understand the fast changing expectations of industry.

- In an interview now the focus is more on what a candidate has achieved in the past as opposed to vague promises of what a candidate can do when recruited.

- The interviewer is looking for employable candidates – who not only meet the required competencies but can also produce the desired results. At the trainee's level the employer is looking whether the candidate has the desired attitude. He should be a achiever and self-motivated person and should display leadership traits.

Make yourself aware of benchmark practices in the field you are working/specialised

- The emphasis today is on variable pay as against a fixed salary. Henceforth selected candidates will be accountable for the pay cheque that they receive. The candidates will have to impress upon the interviewers as to what they can contribute to the organisation and will be accountable for the results and not the time spent in the organisation. In other words today's job seekers have to justify their salary more so than before.

- Organisations are looking for best talents and superior knowledge in specialised fields, as only superior talents will be tomorrow's prime source of competitive advantage. Now 'knowledge employee' is the key word.

- Candidates will have to project to the interviewers that they can contribute for the success of the organisation. For this they will have to develop unique skills and core competencies. People with unique skills will be in great

Learn global trends and develop your unique specialisation and core competencies at least in one field demand as now there is a shift in the focus from lifetime employment to short-term assignments. Candidates should be prepared to accept the job on contract basis or assignment basis.

Do's

1. Develop your unique specialisation and core competencies at least in one field, rather than collecting certificates.
2. In an interview, communicate what you can contribute for the success of the organisation.
3. Learn global trends in your specialised field
4. Be prepared for short-term assignments rather than life long employment.

The greatest things
are accomplished by goal oriented people

ENHANCING YOUR SELF-ESTEEM

By: Mr. Subhash Jagota

Your self-esteem is the most important part of your personality. Everything you do or say or think will affect your self-esteem and help in keeping it high. Self-esteem is the level to which you respect and value yourself as an important, worthwhile person.

To perform your best and to feel terrific about yourself, you should be in a perpetual state of self-esteem building. Just as you take responsibility for your level of physical fitness, you need to take complete responsibility for the content and quality of your mind.

Few simple ways that can help you in enhancing your self-esteem are given below:

1. How much you like and respect yourself is directly affected by your achievements. You have to exploit your potential

If you make others winner,

you are already a winner

to the fullest and learn to fill life with happiness. The very act of aiming high and making written plans of action for their accomplishment raises your self-esteem, and makes you feel much better about yourself.

2. The second element in self-esteem building is having 'clear standards' and 'values' to which you are committed. Men and women with high self-esteem are very clear about what they believe in. The higher your values and ideals are, and the more committed you are to living your life according to those values and ideals, the more you will like and respect yourself, and have high self-esteem.

   "The greatest things are accomplished by goal oriented people"

3. The third element in self-esteem building involves having 'successful experiences'. Once you have set your goals and standards, it is important that you make them

measurable so that you can keep score of your small and large successes along the way. The very act of setting up a goal, breaking it down into smaller parts, and then completing those parts makes you feel like a winner and causes your self-esteem to go up. Remember you cannot feel like a winner unless you clearly lay out the standards by which you are going to measure your success and then achieve those standards.

4. The fourth element of self-esteem is 'comparison with others'. To feel like a winner, you must know for sure that you are doing better than someone else. The more you know about how well the others in your field are doing, and the more favourably you compare with them, the more you will feel like a winner, and the higher your self-esteem will be. Successful people continually compare themselves with other successful people. They think about them, read about them and then work to surpass them.

Success starts the day,
you take decision to succeed with the clear
goal and persistent action plan

You need to take full responsibility for building yourself up on a regular basis. The only way for you to know that you are a valuable and worthwhile person is to make the effort, overcome the obstacles and pay the price to bring these elements into your life. When you have that foundation, you will experience a form of mental fitness and unshakable optimism that will sustain you through failure and propel you to success.

For more details visit:
www.subhashjagota.com

BY THE SAME AUTHOR

FOUNDATION OF SUCCESS

The will to win, the desire to succeed, the urge to reach your full potential is the first step towards your success. This book shares how people can find fulfilment in their family, their work, their community and their faith. Goal Setting is the most important, powerful and fundamental step towards the road to success. This book also covers Scoring High by Goal Setting, Setting Goals-The Family Way, Listing of Dream Goals, Eliminating Stress for Success and exploiting one's potential.

"Mr Subhash Jagota has conveyed in a very simple and practical language, the secret behind success. His varied experience is visible throughout the book. The book makes interesting reading to practitioners, academics, students and those who are beginning their career."

Anil Sachdev, CEO, Grow Talent.Com Ltd

"The author has brought home very ably the need to ignite positive attitude in the workforce in order to be winners in the fast changing competitive global environment."

R L Kapur, Director, Centre for Business Strategies

"Foundation of Success" is a brilliant exposition of Mr Jagota's experience in motivating executives.

N K Bhatt, Chairman, Centre of Labour Education & Social Research

"The chapter on Goal-setting beholds the reader with some very interesting anecdotes and observations borrowed from the real life. It is apparent that author has treated the subject of "Goal Setting" with tremendous belief and conviction."

K K Ahuja, Executive Director, HR, Gujarat Heavy Ind Ltd

"This book has been written in an extremely interesting and readable manner and provide practical guidelines in achieving success."

P C Chatterjee, Chief Executive Group Personnel, DLF Universal Ltd

WINNING STRATEGIES FOR CORPORATE SUCCESS

"Mr Subhash Jagota, in his new book Winning Strategies for Corporate Success, has made an excellent effort by highlighting on various dimensions of an organisation. The author has brought home very ably, the need to ignite positive attitude in the workforce, in order to be winners in the fast changing competitive global environment."

R L Kapur, Director, Centre for Business Strategies

"The book, Winning Strategies for Corporate Success, is an excellent thesis of practical guidelines, to achieve Management Excellence."

Lt Gen M M Walia, PVSM, AVSM, SM (Retd.)

"Mr Subhash Jagota has explained, the whole philosophy of living a peaceful and prosperous life in just one line – If you make others Winners, you are already a Winner. The book indeed has learning material."

Dr Rakesh Chopra, Chairman, Institute of Corporate Management

"I would like to congratulate Mr Subhash Jagota for coming up with a winning book once again! Winning Strategies for Corporate Success is lucid, succinct, relevant and up to date."

Dr Ashwani, CEO, Santulan

"Winning Strategies for Corporate Success is the result of Mr Subhash Jagota's years of experience, which he has shared in the book, in the most lucid way."

Vijay Batra, CEO, Think Inc.

"Winning Strategies for Corporate Success written in an extremely interesting and readable manner, also suggesting ways for creating a Winning Management."

K K Muthu, Former President, Delhi Management Association

For ordering information turn overleaf

ORDER FORM

Yes! I wish to order_______ copy/copies of

- Winning Strategies for Corporate Success
- Foundation of Success
- I enclose a Demand Draft#..................................in favour of Excel Books for Rs. ....
- Please send by VPP

Name____

Designation____

Company____

Address____

____

Tel. No.____

E-mail____

Postage free with all Orders.

Please Mail or Fax to:

EXCEL BOOKS

A-45 Naraina, Phase-1,

New Delhi-110 028, India

Phone: 5795793, 5792799

Fax: 5797221, 3930689

E-mail: info@excelbooks.com